MATERIALS FOR LANGUAGE TEACHING AT RUDOLF STEINER (WALDORF) SCHOOLS

James H. Fassett

The Pancake

Illustrated by
E. H. Shepard
(who also illustrated the 'Winnie the Pooh' books)

New, revised edition
with exercises by Peter Morris

ISBN-10: 3-927286-61-3
ISBN-13: 978-3-927286-61-0

Pädagogische Forschungsstelle beim Bund der Freien Waldorfschulen
Stuttgart 2006

Druck- und Medienzentrum Gerlingen GmbH
Benzstr. 8
70839 Gerlingen

The Key of the Kingdom

This is the Key of the Kingdom:
In that Kingdom is a city,
In that city is a town,
In that town there is a street,
In that street there winds a lane,
In that lane there is a yard,
In that yard there is a house,
In that house there waits a room,
In that room an empty bed,
And on that bed a basket –
A basket of sweet flowers,
Of flowers, of flowers,
A basket of sweet flowers.

Flowers in the basket,
Basket on the bed,
Bed in the chamber,
Chamber in the house,
House in the weedy yard,
Yard in the winding lane,
Lane in the broad street,
Street in the high town,
Town in the city,
City in the Kingdom.

This is the Key of the Kingdom.
Of the Kingdom this is the Key.

Contents

* This poem by an anonymous author has been added for the Rudolf Steiner (Waldorf) School edition. It was not part of the original text.

Seventy-third impression 1990

First Waldorf School edition 1992
Second Waldorf edition, revised and annotated, 2002

The Pancake

A big fat cook was making a big fat pancake.

Near the cook were seven hungry little boys.

"We like big round pancakes, Mr Cook," said all the little boys.

"This pancake will be good to eat," said Mr Cook.

But the pancake in the pan said,

"I will not, not, not be eaten!"

So the big round pancake gave a hop.

The pancake gave a jump.

And off he rolled – out of the pan.

Mr Pancake rolled round and round and round.

And oh! so very, very fast.

"Stop! Stop! Mr Pancake!" said the cook.

But the pancake rolled faster and faster.

Then the big fat cook began to run after the pancake.

"Stop! Stop!" said all the little boys.

But the pancake rolled faster and faster.

Then all the little boys began to run.

The pancake met a little man.

"Stop, Pancake, stop! I am hungry! I want to eat you," said the little man.

"The cook cannot stop me.

The boys cannot stop me.

You cannot stop me," said the pancake, and rolled faster and faster.

Then the little man began to run.

The pancake met a hen.

"Stop, Pancake, stop! I am very hungry!

I want to eat you," said the hen.

"The cook cannot stop me.

The boys cannot stop me.

The man cannot stop me.

You cannot stop me."

And the pancake rolled faster than ever.

Then the hen began to run.

The pancake met a duck.

"Stop, Pancake, stop! I am very, very hungry!

I want to eat you," said the duck.

"The cook cannot stop me.

The boys cannot stop me.

The man cannot stop me.

The hen cannot stop me.

You cannot stop me."

And the pancake rolled faster and faster.

The pancake met a pig.

"Why are you running so fast?" said the pig.

"Can't you see?

The cook, the boys, the man, the hen and the duck all want to eat me."

"That is too bad. I will run with you," said the pig.

So the pig and the pancake went on and on and on.

They came to a wide pond.

"I can't swim," said the pancake.

"I can," said the pig.

"Jump onto my nose, and I will take you across."

So the pancake jumped onto the pig's nose.

The pig gave a big grunt.

And snip! snap! he ate up the big round pancake.

Yes, the pig ate up every bit.

The Old Woman and Her Pig

One day an old woman found a penny.

"What can I do with this penny?" she said.

"I will go to the market and buy a pig."

So the old woman bought a pig.

Then she tied a string to the pig's leg.

On her way home she came to a stile.

The pig would not go over the stile.

She went a little farther and met a dog.

She said to the dog,

"Dog, dog, bite pig;

Pig won't go over stile,
And I shan't get home tonight."
But the dog would not.

She went a little farther and met a stick.

"Stick, stick, beat dog;
Dog won't bite pig,
Pig won't go over stile,
And I shan't get home tonight."

But the stick would not.

She went a little farther and met a fire.

"Fire, fire, burn stick;
Stick won't beat dog,
Dog won't bite pig,
Pig won't go over stile,
And I shan't get home tonight."

But the fire would not.

She went a little farther and met some water.

"Water, water, put out fire;
Fire won't burn stick,
Stick won't beat dog,
Dog won't bite pig,
Pig won't go over stile,
And I shan't get home tonight."

But the water would not.

She went a little farther and met an ox.

"Ox, ox, drink water;
Water won't put out fire,
Fire won't burn stick,
Stick won't beat dog,
Dog won't bite pig,
Pig won't go over stile,
And I shan't get home tonight."

But the ox would not.

She went a little farther and met a man.

"Man, man, kill ox;
Ox won't drink water,
Water won't put out fire,
Fire won't burn stick,
Stick won't beat dog,
Dog won't bite pig,
Pig won't go over stile,
And I shan't get home tonight."
But the man would not.

She went a little farther and met a rope.

"Rope, rope, bind man;
Man won't kill ox,
Ox won't drink water,
Water won't put out fire,
Fire won't burn stick,
Stick won't beat dog,
Dog won't bite pig,
Pig won't go over stile,
And I shan't get home tonight."

But the rope would not.

She went a little farther and met a rat.

"Rat, rat, bite rope;
Rope won't bind man,
Man won't kill ox,
Ox won't drink water,
Water won't put out fire,
Fire won't burn stick,
Stick won't beat dog,
Dog won't bite pig,
Pig won't go over stile,
And I shan't get home tonight."

But the rat would not.

She went a little farther and met a cat.

"Cat, cat, kill rat;
Rat won't bite rope,
Rope won't bind man,
Man won't kill ox,
Ox won't drink water,
Water won't put out fire,
Fire won't burn stick,
Stick won't beat dog,
Dog won't bite pig,
Pig won't go over stile,
And I shan't get home tonight."

The cat said, "You must get me some milk. Then I will kill the rat."

So the old woman went to the cow and said,

"Cow, cow, will you give me some milk?"

The cow said, "Get me a pail of water to drink. Then I will give you some milk."

So the old woman took a pail of water to the cow.

And the cow gave her some milk.

Then the old woman gave the milk to the cat.

The cat began to kill the rat,
The rat began to bite the rope,
The rope began to bind the man,
The man began to kill the ox,
The ox began to drink the water,
The water began to put out the fire,
The fire began to burn the stick,
The stick began to beat the dog,
The dog began to bite the pig,
And the pig jumped over the stile.

So the old woman got home with her pig that night.

The House that Jack Built

This is the house that Jack built.

This is the malt,
That lay in the house that Jack built.

This is the rat,
That ate the malt,
That lay in the house that Jack built.

This is the cat,
That killed the rat,
That ate the malt,
That lay in the house that Jack built.

This is the dog,
That worried the cat,
That killed the rat,
That ate the malt,
That lay in the house that Jack built.

This is the cow with the crumpled horn,
That tossed the dog,
That worried the cat,
That killed the rat,
That ate the malt,
That lay in the house that Jack built.

This is the maiden all forlorn,
That milked the cow with the crumpled
horn,
That tossed the dog,
That worried the cat,
That killed the rat,
That ate the malt,
That lay in the house that Jack built.

This is the man all tattered and torn,
That kissed the maiden all forlorn,
That milked the cow with the crumpled
    horn,
That tossed the dog,
That worried the cat,
That killed the rat,
That ate the malt,
That lay in the house that Jack built.

This is the priest all shaven and shorn,
That married the man all tattered and
torn,
That kissed the maiden all forlorn,
That milked the cow with the crumpled
horn,
That tossed the dog,
That worried the cat,
That killed the rat,
That ate the malt,
That lay in the house that Jack built.

This is the cock that crowed in the
morn,
That woke the priest all shaven and
shorn,
That married the man all tattered and
torn,
That kissed the maiden all forlorn,
That milked the cow with the crumpled
horn,
That tossed the dog,
That worried the cat,
That killed the rat,
That ate the malt,
That lay in the house that Jack built.

This is the farmer sowing his corn,
That kept the cock that crowed in the
morn,
That woke the priest all shaven and
shorn,
That married the man all tattered and
torn,
That kissed the maiden all forlorn,
That milked the cow with the crumpled
horn,
That tossed the dog,
That worried the cat,
That killed the rat,
That ate the malt,
That lay in the house that Jack built.

Dust on the Feather

Oh! the dust on the feather,
And the feather on the bird,
And the bird on the eggs,
And the eggs in the nest,
And the nest on the twig,
And the twig on the branch,
And the branch on the tree,
And the tree in the woods,
And the woods in the ground,
And the green grass grew
All round, round, round,
And the green grass grew all round.

Chicken Licken

Chicken Licken went to the woods one day.

An acorn fell on her little head.

She thought the sky had fallen.

She said, "I will go and tell the king.

I will tell the king that the sky has fallen."

So Chicken Licken turned back and met Hen Len.

"Well, Hen Len, where are you going?"

And Hen Len said,

"I am going to the woods for some food."

Chicken Licken said, "Oh, Hen Len, don't go.

I was going, and the sky fell on my poor little head.

Now I am going to tell the king."

So Hen Len turned back with Chicken Licken.

They met Cock Lock.

"Well, Cock Lock, where are you going?"

And Cock Lock said, "I am going to the woods for some food."

Hen Len said, "Oh, Cock Lock, don't go.

I was going, and I met Chicken Licken.

Chicken Licken was going to the woods.

There the sky fell on her poor little head.

Now we are going to tell the king."

So Cock Lock turned back and met Duck Luck.

"Well, Duck Luck, where are you going?"

Duck Luck said, "I am going to the woods for some food."

Cock Lock said, "Oh, Duck Luck, don't go.

I was going, and I met Hen Len.

Hen Len met Chicken Licken.

Chicken Licken was going to the woods.

There the sky fell on her poor little head.

Now we are going to tell the king."

So Duck Luck turned back and met Drake Lake.

"Well, Drake Lake, where are you going?"

Drake Lake said, "I am going to the woods for some food."

Duck Luck said, "Oh, Drake Lake, don't go.

I was going, and I met Cock Lock.

Cock Lock met Hen Len.

Hen Len met Chicken Licken.

Chicken Licken was going to the woods.

There the sky fell on her poor little head.

Now we are going to tell the king."

So Drake Lake turned back and met Goose Loose.

"Well, Goose Loose, where are you going?"

Goose Loose said, "I am going to the woods for some food."

Drake Lake said, "Oh, Goose Loose, don't go.

I was going, and I met Duck Luck.

Duck Luck met Cock Lock.

Cock Lock met Hen Len.

Hen Len met Chicken Licken.

Chicken Licken was going to the woods.

There the sky fell on her poor little head.

Now we are going to tell the king."

So Goose Loose turned back and met Gander Lander.

"Well, Gander Lander, where are you going?"

Gander Lander said," I am going to the woods for some food."

Goose Loose said, "Oh, Gander Lander, don't go.

I was going, and I met Drake Lake.

Drake Lake met Duck Luck.

Duck Luck met Cock Lock.

Cock Lock met Hen Len.

Hen Len met Chicken Licken.

Chicken Licken was going to the woods.

There the sky fell on her poor little head.

Now we are going to tell the king."

So Gander Lander turned back and met Turkey Lurkey.

"Well, Turkey Lurkey, where are you going?"

Turkey Lurkey said, "I am going to the woods for some food."

Gander Lander said, "Oh, Turkey Lurkey, don't go.

I was going, and I met Goose Loose.

Goose Loose met Drake Lake.

Drake Lake met Duck Luck.

Duck Luck met Cock Lock.

Cock Lock met Hen Len.

Hen Len met Chicken Licken.

Chicken Licken was going to the woods.

There the sky fell on her poor little head.

Now we are going to tell the king."

So Turkey Lurkey turned back.

He walked with Gander Lander.

Goose Loose walked with Drake Lake.

Duck Luck walked with Cock Lock.

Hen Len walked with Chicken Licken.

As they were going along they met Fox Lox.

Fox Lox said, "Where are you all going?"

They said, "Chicken Licken was going to the woods.

The sky fell on her poor little head.

Now we are going to tell the king."

Fox Lox said, "Come with me. I will show you the way to the king."

But Fox Lox took them into his den. He and his little foxes soon ate up poor Chicken Licken, Hen Len, Cock Lock, Duck Luck, Drake Lake, Goose Loose, Gander Lander, and Turkey Lurkey.

So they never saw the king.

And they never told him that the sky had fallen.

The Three Billy Goats Gruff

Once upon a time there were three goats.

The first was Little Billy Goat Gruff.

The second was Big Billy Goat Gruff.

The third was Great Big Billy Goat Gruff.

The three goats lived in a field.

In the field there ran a little river.

Across this river there was a bridge.

Now under this bridge there lived a wicked dwarf.

This dwarf liked to eat goats better than anything else.

So the three goats did not dare step on the bridge.

But on the other side of the river the grass was fresh and green.

There were ripe berries and good red apples, too.

How the three goats longed to cross that bridge!

They wanted to eat the grass, and the berries, and the apples.

But they were afraid of the wicked dwarf under the bridge.

One day Little Billy Goat Gruff said, "I will cross that bridge.

I am going to eat some of that rich green grass."

"If you do, the dwarf will catch you," said the other goats.

"I am not afraid," said Little Billy Goat Gruff. "He will not eat me. I am too little."

So off he trotted, trip-trap, trip-trap, over the bridge.

"Who is running trip-trap, trip-trap, over my bridge?" said the wicked dwarf.

"It is I, Little Billy Goat Gruff."

"Then I will eat you," said the dwarf.

"No, do not eat me. I am too little.

Eat Big Billy Goat Gruff when he comes over the bridge.

He is much fatter than I am."

"Very well," said the dwarf. "You may run over my bridge."

So Little Billy Goat Gruff ran trip-trap, trip-trap, over the bridge.

Big Billy Goat Gruff saw Little Billy Goat Gruff run over the bridge.

He saw him begin to eat the rich green grass.

Then Big Billy Goat Gruff said,

"I will run over the bridge too.

The dwarf did not eat Little Billy Goat Gruff.

So he will not eat me."

Soon he trotted trip-trap, trip-trap, over the bridge.

"Who is trotting trip-trap, trip-trap, over my bridge?" said the wicked dwarf.

"It is I, Big Billy Goat Gruff."

"Then I will eat you," said the dwarf.

"No, do not eat me," said Big Billy Goat Gruff.

"Eat Great Big Billy Goat Gruff when he comes over the bridge.

He is much fatter than I am."

"Very well," said the dwarf. "You may run over my bridge."

Then Great Big Billy Goat Gruff saw Big Billy Goat Gruff and Little Billy Goat Gruff eating the rich green grass.

He saw them eating the ripe berries and the red apples.

Great Big Billy Goat Gruff said,

"I will run over the bridge too.

The dwarf did not eat Big Billy Goat Gruff.

He did not eat Little Billy Goat Gruff.

So he will not eat me."

Then Great Big Billy Goat Gruff went over the bridge, trip-trap, trip-trap.

"Who is going trip-trap, trip-trap, over my bridge?" said the wicked dwarf.

"It is I, Great Big Billy Goat Gruff."

"Ah! Then I will eat you up," said the dwarf.

"Come up here and try it," said Great Big Billy Goat Gruff.

So the wicked dwarf gave a jump, and there he was on the bridge.

Great Big Billy Goat Gruff was not afraid.

He shook his horns and stamped his feet.

The wicked dwarf began to be afraid.

Then Great Big Billy Goat Gruff ran at the dwarf.

He ran as hard as he could run.

His sharp horns caught the wicked dwarf, and tossed him right off the bridge.

Down, down went the dwarf into the deep, deep water.

"Ho! Ho! You would eat me, would you?" said Great Big Billy Goat Gruff.

"Now you can drink water instead."

So Great Big Billy Goat Gruff, Big Billy Goat Gruff, and Little Billy Goat Gruff ate the green grass, the ripe berries, and the red apples.

And all three of them grew fat, on the other side of the river.

The Goat Boy

Once upon a time there was a little boy who lived on a farm.

His father had a flock of goats.

Each morning the boy drove the goats to a hillside to feed.

One day the goats jumped over a fence into a field of turnips.

The boy tried to drive the goats out, but they would not go.

So the boy sat down on a stone and began to cry.

Mr Rabbit came along.

"Hello, little boy. Why are you crying?" said Mr Rabbit.

"I am crying because I can't drive the goats out of the field."

"Ho! If that's all, I'll do it," said Mr Rabbit.

So he tried to drive the goats out of the turnip field, but they would not go.

Then Mr Rabbit sat down on a stone and began to cry.

Pretty soon, along came Mr Fox.

"Hello, Mr Rabbit, why are you crying?" said Mr Fox.

"I am crying because the boy is crying.

The boy is crying because he can't drive the goats out of the turnip field."

"Ho, ho! If that's all, I'll do it," said Mr Fox.

So he tried to drive the goats out of the turnip field, but they would not go.

Then Mr Fox sat down on a stone and began to cry.

Soon Mr Wolf came along.

"Hello, Mr Fox, why are you crying?" said Mr Wolf.

"I am crying because Mr Rabbit is crying.

Mr Rabbit is crying because the boy is crying.

And the boy is crying because he can't drive the goats out of the turnip field."

"Ho, ho, ho! If that's all, I'll do it," said Mr Wolf.

So he tried to drive the goats out of the turnip field, but they would not go.

Then Mr Wolf sat down on a stone and began to cry.

While they were all sitting on the stones crying, little Mrs Bee came buzzing along.

"Hello, Mr Wolf, why are you crying?" said Mrs Bee.

"I am crying because Mr Fox is crying.

Mr Fox is crying because Mr Rabbit is crying.

Mr Rabbit is crying because the boy is crying.

And the boy is crying because he can't drive the goats out of the turnip field."

"Buzz, buzz, buzz! If that's all, I'll do it," said Mrs Bee.

Then Mr Wolf and Mr Fox and Mr Rabbit and the boy all stopped crying.

They began to make fun of Mrs Bee.

"You? You can't do it!" they all cried.

Little Mrs Bee said nothing.

She flew into the turnip field and stung Great Big Billy Goat.

Out of the turnip field ran Great Big Billy Goat and all the other goats ran after him.

Little Half-Chick

Once upon a time there was an old mother hen.

She had five little chicks.

Four of these chicks were just like other little chicks.

They had two little legs, two little wings, and two bright little eyes.

But the fifth little chick had only one little leg, one little wing, and one little eye.

He could not run and jump like his little brothers and sisters.

He had to go hoppity-skip, hoppity-skip, hoppity-skip.

Little Half-Chick did not care in the least.

He felt proud of his one leg, his one wing, and his one eye.

He felt proud that he was not like his little brothers and sisters.

He went about, hoppity-skip, hoppity-skip, very proud indeed.

One day he said to his mother,

"I am tired of this old farm yard.

I am going to see the king."

So off he went, hoppity-skip, hoppity-skip, to find the king's palace.

He had not gone far when he came to a little brook.

The little brook was very sad.

It was so full of grass and twigs that the water could not flow.

"Help me, help me, dear little Half-Chick," cried the water.

"Why should I help you?" cried proud little Half-Chick.

Soon Half-Chick came to a fire.

The fire was made of damp wood.

It was smoking and almost out.

"Help me, help me, dear little Half-Chick," cried the fire.

"Fan me with your little wing, so that I shall blaze again."

"Why should I help you? You can never help me," cried Half-Chick.

So on he went, hoppity-skip, hoppity-skip, to see the king.

When Half-Chick came to the king's palace, he met the king's cook.

"Ho, ho!" said the cook. "What a queer chick!

It will make a good dinner for the king."

So he took Half-Chick and put him into a pot of water.

Then he put the pot of water onto the fire.

"Oh!" cried little Half-Chick. "Do not cover my head, water, or I shall drown."

"Why should I help you?" cried the water.

"You did not help me."

Then the water bubbled over Half-Chick's head.

Soon the water grew hotter and hotter.

"Please, fire," cried little Half-Chick, "do not heat the water, or I shall burn."

"Why should I help you?" cried the fire.

"You did not help me."

And the fire burned and burned.

The cook soon came to take Half-Chick out of the pot for the king's dinner.

He lifted the lid of the pot and looked in.

"Ah!" said the cook. "This chick will never do for the king's dinner.

The fire was too hot. It has burned him to a crisp."

Then he took Half-Chick by his one leg, and tossed him through an open window.

The wind took him and blew him to the top of the highest steeple.

There little Half-Chick stays, even to this day, with his one leg, and his one wing, and his one eye.

Can you see him turn and turn as the wind blows?

The Gingerbread Boy

Once upon a time there lived a little old woman and a little old man.

They lived in a little old house down under a hill.

These two lived all alone in the little old house.

They had no little boys and no little girls.

One day the little old woman said,

"I will make a boy out of gingerbread.

I will make sugar frosting for his coat.

I will make his eyes and mouth out of bits of sugar candy.

His nose I will make out of a big fat currant.

I will make his shoes out of nuts."

So the little old woman cut out his toes.

She patted out his legs and his arms.

She put him in a pan.

Then she put the gingerbread boy into the oven to bake.

"Oho!" she cried. "Now I shall have a little gingerbread boy of my own."

Then she went about her work.

Soon it was time for the gingerbread boy to come out of the oven.

As she went to the oven, she heard a tiny little voice.

It said, "Let me out! Let me out!"

The little old woman ran to open the oven door.

What do you think?

Out popped the little gingerbread boy.

He ran hopping and skipping across the floor.

Seeing the open door, out he went.

Down the street ran the gingerbread boy.

After him ran the little old woman and the little old man.

"Stop! Stop! Gingerbread Boy!" they called.

But he only looked back and cried,

"Run, run, as fast as you can.

You can't catch me.

I'm the gingerbread man."

And they could not catch him.

The little gingerbread boy ran on and on.

Soon he came to a cow.

"Stop! Stop! Little boy!" said the cow.

"You look very good to eat."

But he only ran the faster and cried,

"I have run away from a little old woman and a little old man.

I can run away from you, I can.

Run, run, as fast as you can.

You can't catch me.

I'm the gingerbread man."

And the cow could not catch him.

The gingerbread boy ran on and on.

Soon he met a horse.

"Stop! Stop! Little Gingerbread Boy!" cried the horse.

"You look very good to eat."

But he only ran the faster, and looking back, he cried,

"I have run away from a little old woman and a little old man and a cow.

I can run away from you, I can.

Run, run, as fast as you can.

You can't catch me.
I'm the gingerbread man."

And the horse tried to catch him, but he could not.

Now the little gingerbread boy began to be very proud of his running.

He said, "No one can catch me."

Just then he met a sly old fox.

And the fox said,

"Wait a bit, little Gingerbread Boy. I want to talk to you."

"Oho! You can't catch me," said the gingerbread boy.

Then the fox began to run, and the gingerbread boy began to run.

Then the fox ran faster, and the gingerbread boy ran faster.

As he ran, he looked back and cried,

"I have run away from a little old woman, a little old man, a cow, and a horse.

I can run away from you, I can.

Run, run, as fast as you can.

You can't catch me.

I'm the gingerbread man."

"Why," said the fox, "I don't want to catch you.

I want to help you."

But the gingerbread boy kept on running.

And the fox kept on running.

Soon they came to a river.

"Oh! What shall I do?" cried the gingerbread boy.

"I can't cross the river."

"Jump onto my tail," said the fox.

"I will take you across."

So the gingerbread boy jumped onto the fox's tail.

The fox began to swim across the river.

Soon the fox turned his head and said, "You are too heavy for my tail.

You will get wet.

Jump onto my back."

So the little gingerbread boy jumped onto the fox's back.

Then the fox swam a little farther out into the river.

"Dear little Gingerbread Boy," he said, "my back is sinking.

You will get wet.

Jump onto my nose."

So the little gingerbread boy jumped onto the fox's nose.

Soon the fox's feet touched the bank of the river.

He tossed the gingerbread boy into the air.

He opened his mouth, and snap! went his teeth.

"Dear me," said the little gingerbread boy. "I am a quarter gone."

Then he said, "Why, I am half gone."

Then he cried, "I am three quarters gone."

And after that the little gingerbread boy said nothing at all.

Exercises

Some Tips for Teachers

- ✧ The biggest problem most children face with exercises like these is not the questions themselves, but the fact that they are written, and that the teacher may expect written answers.
- ✧ So the golden rule for teachers is: ***Do everything orally first!*** This means: ***Only the teacher*** *has the page of questions in front of him.* If the children know the story well, they can give all (or most of) the answers without using their books.
- ✧ A second stage is for the children to give the answer, and then look for the corresponding place in the text.
- ✧ Later, books can be open at the exercise pages, with the teacher reading the questions. How the children should answer now is a matter for the teacher's judgement:
  - — Answering without looking at the text helps fluency and self-confidence, and is easiest with well-practised stories;
  - — Checking the text and looking for the answers in stories that the class doesn't know so well practises the first methods of individual work, and thus helps to lay the groundwork for what the Middle School will bring.
- ✧ Giving exercises as oral or written homework should thus be seen as an **advanced** stage in the learning sequence, and **not** as an introduction to this kind of work.
- ✧ A wide range of exercises is offered so that the teacher can pick what seems most useful for the individual class.

THE PANCAKE

Exercise 1— Who (page 5)

1. Who was making a big fat pancake?
2. Who was near the cook?
3. Who likes big round pancakes?
4. Who said, "This pancake will be good to eat"?
5. Who said, "I will not, not, not be eaten"?

Exercise 2 — Short Answers (page 5)

1. Was a big fat cook making a pancake?
2. Was the pancake in the pan?
3. Did he say, "Please eat me"?
4. Did he roll out of the pan?

Exercise 3 — Who and What (page 6)

1. What did the cook say?
2. Who rolled faster and faster?
3. Who began to run after the pancake then?
4. What did all the little boys say?

Exercise 4 — Describing a Picture (page 6)

1. What can you see in the picture on page 6? Make up at least four sentences.

Exercise 5 — Who (page 7)

1. Who began to run now?
2. Who met a little man?
3. Who is hungry?
4. Who wants to eat the pancake?
5. Who can't stop the pancake?

Exercise 6 — Either/Or (page 5)

1. Was the cook fat or thin?
2. Were the boys big or little?
3. Were the boys near the cook or outside the house?
4. Did the pancake roll out of the pan or into it?

Exercise 7 — Finding Words (page 5)

1. What is the opposite of *little?*
2. What is the opposite of *thin?*
3. What is the next number after *six?*
4. What is the opposite of *bad?*
5. What is the opposite of *into?*

Exercise 8 — Who (pages 8–9)

1. Who said, "I am very hungry"?
2. Who can't stop the pancake?
3. Who rolled faster than ever?
4. Who began to run now?
5. Who said, "I am very, very hungry"?
6. Who can you see in the picture on page 9?

Exercise 9 — Put into the Past Tense (pages 8–9)

1. The pancake *meets* a hen.
2. "I want to eat you," *says* the hen.
3. The pancake *rolls* faster and faster.
4. The hen *begins* to run.
5. "I am very, very hungry!" *says* the duck.

Exercise 10 — Short Answers (pages 8–9)

1. Did the pancake meet a hen?
2. Did the hen say, "Stop, Pancake, stop!"?
3. Did the pancake roll faster than ever?
4. Can the cook stop the pancake?
5. Can the boys stop the pancake?

Exercise 11 — Describing a Picture (page 8)

1. What can you see in the picture on page 8? Make up at least five sentences.

Exercise 12 — Who and What (pages 10–11)

1. Who did the pancake meet after the duck?
2. What did the pig say?
3. Who came to a wide pond?
4. What did the pancake jump onto?
5. Who gave a big grunt?

Exercise 13 — Short Answers (pages 10–11)

1. Did the pancake meet a pig now?
2. Did the pig say, "I want to eat you"?
3. Did the pig and the pancake come to a little house?
4. Did they come to a wide pond?
5. Did the pig eat up the big round pancake?

Exercise 14 — Either/Or (pages 10–11)

1. Did the pancake meet a pig or a farmer?
2. Did the pig run with the boys or the pancake?
3. Did they come to a house or to a pond?
4. Who can swim - the pig or the pancake?

5. Did the pig give a hop, or a jump, or a big grunt?
6. Who ate up the pancake - the pig or the duck?

Exercise 15 — Put into the Past Tense (pages 10–11)

1. The pancake *meets* a pig.
2. The pig and the pancake *come* to a wide pond.
3. The pancake *jumps* onto the pig's nose.
4. The pig *gives* a big grunt.
5. He *eats* up the big round pancake.

Exercise 16 — Describing a Picture (page 11)

1. What can you see in the picture on page 11? Make up at least five sentences.

THE OLD WOMAN AND HER PIG

Exercise 17 — What (page 13)

1. What did an old woman find one day?
2. What did she say?
3. What did she buy at the market?
4. What did she tie to the pig's leg?
5. What did she come to, on her way home?
6. What would the pig not do?
7. What did the old woman meet, a little farther on?
8. What did she say to the dog?

Exercise 18 — Put into the Past Tense (page 13)

1. One day an old woman *finds* a penny.
2. "What can I do with this penny?" she *says.*
3. The old woman *buys* a pig.
4. She *ties* a string to the pig's leg.
5. On her way home she *comes* to a stile.
6. The pig *will* not go over the stile.
7. The old woman *goes* a little farther.
8. She *meets* a dog.
9. She *says* to the dog, "Dog, dog, bite pig."

Exercise 19 — Short Answers (pages 14–15)

1. Would the dog bite the pig?
2. Did the old woman go a little farther?
3. Did she meet a stick?
4. Did she say, "Pig, pig, eat pancake"?
5. Would the stick beat the dog?
6. Did the old woman meet a fire now?
7. Did she say, "I am very, very hungry"?
8. Would the fire burn the stick?

Exercise 20 — Describing a Picture (page 15)

1. What can you see in the picture on page 15? Write at least five sentences.

Exercise 21 — Finding Words (pages 13–15)

1. What is the opposite of *night?*
2. What is the opposite of *young?*
3. What is the opposite of *man?*
4. What is the word for a *big fat farm animal that grunts?*
5. What is the *animal that barks, "Bow-wow!"?*
6. What is burning in the picture on page 15?
7. The pig is sleeping next to a ......
8. Stick won't ...... dog.
9. Dog won't ...... pig.
10. I shan't get home ......

Exercise 22 — Either/Or (pages 16–17)

1. What did the woman meet now - a big fat cook or some water?
2. What should put out the fire - the water or the stick?
3. What should the fire burn - the stick or the stile?
4. What should the dog bite - the old woman's shoe or the pig?
5. What did the old woman meet now - an ox or a hen?
6. Should the ox bite the pig or drink the water?

7. Should the stick beat the pig or the dog?
8. In the picture on page 17, is the ox standing in a field or in the water?

Exercise 23 — What (page 18)

1. What should the man kill?
2. What should the ox drink?
3. What should put out the fire?
4. What should the fire burn?
5. What should the stick beat?
6. What should bite the pig?
7. What should go over the stile?
8. What won't the pig go over?

Exercise 24 — Missing Words (page 19)

1. She ...... a little farther.
2. She ...... a rope.
3. Rope, rope, ... man.
4. Ox won't ...... water.
5. Water won't .... fire.
6. Fire won't ...... stick.
7. Stick ...... beat dog.
8. Pig won't .... stile.

Exercise 25 — Either/Or (page 20)

1. Should the rat bite the rope or the pig?
2. What won't the rope bind - the man or the ox?
3. What won't drink the water - the ox or the dog?
4. What wouldn't bite the rope - the dog, the rat or the pig?

Exercise 26 — Puzzles (pages 13–21)

1. Which animal drinks milk and kills rats?
2. What can we drink, and can put out fire?
3. Which animal in this story eats grass?
4. Which animals in this story eat other animals?

5. Two things here can *tie* or *bind* - what are they?
6. Which animals in the story do many people like to have in their houses?
7. Which animals in the story would you not like to find sleeping in your bedroom?
8. Which is the smallest animal in the story?
9. Which is the biggest animal in the story?
10. Which is the fattest animal in the story?

Exercise 27 — Short Answers (page 22)

1. Did the old woman go to the cow now?
2. Did she ask the cow for some milk?
3. Did the cow ask for some water to drink?
4. Did she say, "Then I will jump over the stile"?
5. Did the old woman give the cow a pail of water?
6. Did the old woman beat the cow?
7. Did the cow give her some milk?
8. Did the cow bite the old woman?

Exercise 28 — Describing a Picture (page 22)

1. What can you see in the picture on page 22? Make up at least five sentences.

Exercise 29 — What (page 23)

1. What did the old woman give the cat?
2. What did the rat begin to bite?
3. What began to put out the fire?
4. What did the fire begin to burn?
5. What began to bite the pig?
6. What did the pig do?

THE HOUSE THAT JACK BUILT

Exercise 30 — Describing a Picture (page 24)

1. What can you see in the picture on page 24? Make up at least five sentences.

Exercise 31 — Rhyming Words (pages 24–25)

1. What word rhymes with *miss?*
2. What word rhymes with *mouse?*
3. What word rhymes with *smack?*
4. What word rhymes with *tilt?*
5. What word rhymes with *salt?*
6. What word rhymes with *say?*
7. What word rhymes with *hat?*
8. What word rhymes with *late?*

Exercise 32 — Looking at Pictures (pages 26–27)

In the pictures on pages 26 and 27 ...

1. What can you see in the cat's mouth?
2. What can you see that is brown?
3. What can you see that is green?
4. What can you see that has horns?
5. What can you see that has four legs?
6. Is the cow running after the dog, or is the dog running after the cow?
7. What is the dog doing on page 26?
8. Which animal is not running in these pictures?

Exercise 33 — Looking at Pictures (pages 28–29)

In the pictures on pages 28 and 29 ...

1. What colour is the maiden's dress?
2. What colour are the bushes?
3. What colour is the side of the house on page 28?
4. What colour are the three geese?
5. What colour is the man's jacket?
6. What colour is the sky on page 29?
7. Where is the man's hat?

Exercise 34 — Either/Or (pages 30–31)

1. Is the priest forlorn or shaven and shorn?
2. Is the man shaven and shorn or tattered and torn?

3. Is a maiden a boy or a girl?
4. What gives us milk - a cow or a cat?
5. Did the cow toss the cat or the dog?
6. Did the cat kill a rat or a pig?
7. Was the malt in Jack's house or in the garden?
8. Did the cock crow at night or in the morning?

Exercise 35 — Short Answers (page 32)

1. Is the farmer sowing his corn?
2. Did the cock crow in the morning?
3. Was the priest all shaven and shorn?
4. Was the man all forlorn?
5. Did the man kiss the maiden?
6. Did he milk the cow?
7. Did the maiden milk the cow?
8. Did she toss the dog?

CHICKEN LICKEN

Exercise 36 — Who, Where and What (page 35)

1. Where did Chicken Licken go one day?
2. What fell on her head?
3. What did she think had fallen?
4. Who will she go and tell?
5. Who did she meet when she turned back?
6. Where was Hen Len going?
7. What did Hen Len want to find in the woods?
8. What did Chicken Licken say to Hen Len?

Exercise 37 — Short Answers (pages 36–37)

1. Was Chicken Licken going to the woods?
2. Is she going to tell the king now?
3. Did Hen Len turn back with Chicken Licken?
4. Did they meet Cock Lock?
5. Was Cock Lock going to the woods for some food?
6. Did Hen Len say, "Oh, Cock Lock, don't go" ?

7. Was Hen Len going to jump over a stile?
8. Did Cock Lock roll faster and faster?

Exercise 38 — Either/Or (pages 38–39)

1. Was Duck Luck going home or to the woods?
2. Did Cock Lock say, "Don't go" or "Stop! I am hungry"?
3. Did Hen Len meet Chicken Licken or the king?
4. Was Chicken Licken going to school or to the woods?
5. Did the sky [seem to] fall on Chicken Licken's head or on the teacher's head?
6. Did Duck Luck meet a pancake or Drake Lake?
7. Did Duck Luck say, "Oh, Drake Lake, don't go" or "I am going to the king for some food"?
8. Who said, "Goose Loose, where are you going?" - Duck Luck or Drake Lake?

Exercise 39 — Who (pages 40–41)

1. Who said, "Oh, Goose Loose, don't go"?
2. Who met Cock Lock?
3. Who did Hen Len meet?
4. Who are all the animals going to tell?
5. Who did Goose Loose meet?
6. Who said, "I am going to the woods for some food"?
7. Who said, "Oh, Gander Lander, don't go"?
8. Who met Drake Lake?

Exercise 40 — Finding Words (pages 42–43)

1. Lots of trees here! The word begins with 'w'.
2. In summer, this is often blue! It begins with 's'.
3. He has a crown on his head, and his word begins with 'k'.
4. The biggest bird on the farm. It begins with 't'.
5. The things I eat are my ...... (It begins with 'f'.)
6. Young hen, baby hen. It begins with 'ch'.
7. This means 'go, but not run'. It begins with 'w'.

Exercise 41 — Describing Pictures (pages 44–45)

1. What can you see in the pictures on pages 44 and 45? Make up at least six sentences.

Exercise 42 — Who, What and Where (pages 44–45)

1. Who did they meet as they were going along?
2. Where are all the animals going?
3. What did Fox Lox say to the animals?
4. Where did he take them?
5. Who ate up all the animals?
6. Who never saw the king?
7. What did they never tell the king?

THE THREE BILLY GOATS GRUFF

Exercise 43 — Who and Where (page 47)

1. Who was the first goat?
2. Who was the third goat?
3. Where did the three goats live?
4. Where was the bridge?
5. Who lived under the bridge?
6. Where did the dwarf live?

Exercise 44 — Either/Or (pages 48–49)

1. Where was the grass fresh and green - on the goats' side of the river or on the other side?
2. Did the dwarf want to eat the apples, or the goats?
3. Which goat crossed the bridge first - Little Billy Goat Gruff or Big Billy Goat Gruff?
4. Why was Little Billy Goat Gruff not afraid - because he was big or because he was little?
5. Did he trot over the bridge or into the river?
6. Did the dwarf live on the bridge or under the bridge?

Exercise 45 — What, Where and Why (pages 48–49)

1. Where was the grass fresh and green?
2. What did the three goats long to cross?

3. What did they want to eat?
4. Where was the wicked dwarf?
5. What did the other goats say to Little Billy Goat Gruff?
6. Why will the dwarf not eat Little Billy Goat Gruff?

Exercise 46 — Who (pages 50–51)

1. Who is much fatter than Little Billy Goat Gruff?
2. Who said, "You may run over my bridge"?
3. Who began to eat the rich green grass?
4. Who will run over the bridge now?
5. Who spoke to Big Billy Goat Gruff?
6. Who is much fatter than Big Billy Goat Gruff?

Exercise 47 — Short Answers (pages 50–51)

1. Did the dwarf eat Little Billy Goat Gruff?
2. Is Little Billy Goat Gruff much fatter than Big Billy Goat Gruff?
3. Did Little Billy Goat Gruff begin to eat the rich grass?
4. Did Big Billy Goat Gruff trot trip-trap, trip-trap, over the bridge?
5. Could the dwarf see Big Billy Goat Gruff?
6. Was the dwarf bigger than Big Billy Goat Gruff?

Exercise 48 — Put into the Past Tense (pages 52–53)

1. Great Big Billy Goat Gruff *sees* the other goats eating.
2. He *says*, "I will run over the bridge too."
3. So he *goes* over the bridge.
4. The wicked dwarf *gives* a jump onto the bridge.
5. Great Big Billy Goat Gruff *stamps* his feet.
6. Then he *runs* at the dwarf.

Exercise 49 — Missing Words (pages 52–53)

1. I ...... run over the ...... too.
2. The dwarf ...... not ...... Big Billy Goat Gruff.
3. So he ...... not eat ....
4. Great ...... Billy Goat Gruff ...... not afraid.

5. He ...... his horns and stamped his ......
6. The ...... dwarf began to be ....

Exercise 50 — Who, What and Where (pages 54–55)

1. What caught the wicked dwarf?
2. Who did Great Big Billy Goat Gruff toss off the bridge?
3. Where did the dwarf fall?
4. What can the dwarf drink now?
5. Who ate the grass, the berries and the apples?
6. Where did all three goats grow fat?

Exercise 51 — Describing Pictures (pages 46–55)

1. There are seven pictures for this story, appearing between pages 46 and 55. Try and make up a different sentence for each picture!
2. A more difficult task: How many sentences can you make up for the seven pictures? They should all be different, and not just *"I can see the apples"* next to *"I can see the red apples"*!

THE GOAT BOY

Exercise 52 — Who, What and Where (page 57)

1. Who lived on a farm?
2. What did the boy's father have?
3. Where did the boy drive the goats each morning?
4. What did the goats jump over one day?
5. Who tried to drive the goats out?
6. Where did the boy sit down?
7. Who came along now?
8. Why is the boy crying?

Exercise 53 — Short Answers (pages 58–59)

1. Did the boy try to drive the goats into a house?
2. Would the goats go out of the field?
3. Did Mr Rabbit beat the goats with a stick?
4. Did Mr Fox try to drive the goats out?

5. Did they go?
6. Did Mr Wolf come along now?

Exercise 54 — Put into the Past Tense (pages 60–61)

1. Mr Wolf *tries* to drive the goats out of the field.
2. Then Mr Wolf *sits* down on a stone.
3. He *begins* to cry.
4. Now little Mrs Bee *comes* buzzing along.
5. Mr Wolf and Mr Fox and Mr Rabbit and the boy all *stop* crying.
6. Little Mrs Bee *says* nothing.
7. She *flies* into the turnip field.
8. She *stings* Great Big Billy Goat.

Exercise 55 — Puzzles

1. Which animal in the story has long ears and a white tail?
2. Which animals in the story like to eat other animals?
3. How many animals do you know that have horns?
4. What is the opposite of *laughing?*
5. How many things do you know *(outside the story!)* that goats like to eat?
6. How many things do you know *(outside the story!)* that people like to eat?

LITTLE HALF-CHICK

Exercise 56 — Short Answers (page 63)

1. Did the old mother hen have five little chicks?
2. Was the fifth chick just like other little chicks?
3. Could he run like his brothers and sisters?
4. Could he jump like his brothers and sisters?
5. Did he go hoppity-skip, hoppity-skip?

Exercise 57 — Either/Or (pages 64–65)

1. Was little Half-Chick proud that he was not like his brothers and sister, or was he sad?

2. Was Half-Chick going to the woods for some food, or was he going to see the king?
3. Did he come to a little brook or to a field of turnips?
4. Was the little brook very sad, or very hungry?
5. Did Half-Chick come to a fire now, or to a stile?
6. Was the fire made of grass or of damp wood?

Exercise 58 — Rhyming Words (pages 66–67)

1. What word rhymes with *book?*
2. What word rhymes with *thick?*
3. What word rhymes with *sing?*
4. What word rhymes with *hot?*
5. What word rhymes with *bed* and *said?*
6. What word rhymes with *moon?*
7. What word rhymes with *bake?*

Exercise 59 — Who, What and Where (pages 66–69)

1. Who did Half-Chick meet at the king's palace?
2. Where did the cook put Half-Chick?
3. Where did he put the pot of water?
4. What bubbled over Half-Chick's head?
5. Who came to take Half-Chick out of the pot?
6. What was too hot and burned Half-Chick?
7. What blew Half-Chick to the top of the steeple?

Exercise 60 — Describing Pictures (pages 68–69)

1. What can you see in the pictures on pages 68 and 69? Make up at least five sentences.

THE GINGERBREAD BOY

Exercise 61 — Short Answers (page 71)

1. Did the little old woman live in a little old house?
2. Did the little old man live in a field of turnips?
3. Was the little old house down under a hill?
4. Did the two old people live all alone in the house?

5. Did they have any little boys and girls?
6. Will the old woman make a boy out of gingerbread?
7. Will she make his eyes and mouth out of gingerbread?

Exercise 62 — Looking at a Picture (page 70)

In the picture on page 70 ...

1. What has the old woman got in her hands?
2. What is the cat doing?
3. Where is the man working?
4. What can you see that is green?
5. What can you see that is red?
6. What can you see that is brown?
7. What can you see that is blue?
8. How many doors are open?

Exercise 63 — Either/Or (pages 72–73)

1. Will the old woman make the gingerbread boy's shoes out of nuts or sugar candy?
2. Did she put him in a pan or a pot of water?
3. Did she put him into the oven to bake or to sing songs?
4. Was the voice from the oven big and loud or tiny and little?
5. What did the old woman run to open - the oven door or the door of the house?
6. Did the gingerbread boy run down the street or over a bridge?

Exercise 64 — Looking at a Picture (page 73)

In the picture on page 73 ...

1. Who has got a spoon in her hand?
2. Where is the old man's hand?
3. What is the gingerbread boy doing?
4. What can you see that is green?
5. What can you see that is red?
6. What can you see that is brown?
7. How many windows can you see?

Exercise 65 — Who and What (pages 74–75)

1. Who cried, "You can't catch me"?
2. Who said, "Stop! Stop! Little boy!"?
3. Who only ran the faster?
4. Who has the gingerbread boy run away from?
5. Who did the gingerbread boy meet after the cow?
6. What did the horse cry?

Exercise 66 — Put into the Past Tense (pages 76–77)

1. The horse *tries* to catch the gingerbread boy.
2. The gingerbread boy *begins* to be very proud.
3. Then he *meets* a sly old fox.
4. "Oho! You can't catch me," *says* the gingerbread boy.
5. The gingerbread boy and the fox *keep* on running.
6. Soon they *come* to a river.

Exercise 67 — Mixed Questions (pages 78–79)

1. Who said, "Jump onto my tail"?
2. Did the gingerbread boy jump onto the fox's tail?
3. What did the fox begin to do?
4. Did the gingerbread boy jump onto the fox's back?
5. Who said, "Jump onto my nose"?
6. What soon touched the bank of the river?
7. Did the fox toss the gingerbread boy into the river?
8. Did he eat the little gingerbread boy?

Exercise 68 — Missing Words (pages 78–79)

1. "Jump onto my tail," said the fox. "I will ...... you across."
2. The fox began to swim ...... the river.
3. "You are too heavy for my tail. You will get ......"
4. The gingerbread boy jumped ...... the fox's back.
5. Soon the fox's feet touched the ...... of the river.
6. He tossed the gingerbread boy into the ......
7. He ...... his mouth, and snap! went his teeth.
8. After that the little gingerbread boy said ...... at all.

List of English Irregular Verbs

Introduction

Here is a list of the most important English irregular verbs, arranged not alphabetically, but in 'sound families', as experience has shown that this helps learning. Most classes will master the whole list by the end of Class 8; at earlier stages, the individual teacher will select what is to be learned.

Here, then, the teacher can choose material according to the specific needs of the class, while still giving each pupil an overview of the material to be covered in the course of the following years.

The 48 irregular verbs occurring in the main text of this reader are marked with an asterisk before the verb number.

GROUP 1 – BEGIN

*	1.	to begin	began	begun	anfangen
	2.	to spring	sprang	sprung	(plötzlich) springen
	3.	to sing	sang	sung	singen
	4.	to ring	rang	rung	läuten, anrufen
*	5.	to swim	swam	swum	schwimmen
*	6.	to drink	drank	drunk	trinken
*	7.	to sink	sank	sunk	sinken, versenken
	8.	to stink	stank	stunk	stinken

GROUP 2 – CLING

	9.	to cling	clung	clung	s. anklammern, festhalten
*	10.	to sting	stung	stung	stechen
	11.	to fling	flung	flung	schleudern
	12.	to swing	swung	swung	schwingen, schwenken; baumeln
	13.	to wring	wrung	wrung	(aus)wringen
	14.	to hang	hung (hanged = henkte, erhängt!)	hung	(auf)hängen
	15.	to spin	spun	spun	sich drehen, *(Garn)* spinnen
	16.	to dig	dug	dug	graben
	17.	to stick	stuck	stuck	(an)stecken, ankleben
	18.	to strike	struck	struck	schlagen, treffen
	19.	to win	won	won	gewinnen

GROUP 3 – SLEEP

	20.	to sleep	slept	slept	schlafen
	21.	to creep	crept	crept	kriechen
	22.	to sweep	swept	swept	fegen, kehren
*	23.	to keep	kept	kept	behalten

	24. to weep	wept	wept	weinen
*	25. to meet	met	met	treffen, begegnen
*	26. to feel	felt	felt	(sich) fühlen
	27. to kneel	knelt	knelt	knien
	28. to bleed	bled	bled	bluten
*	29. to feed	fed	fed	füttern
	30. to flee	fled	fled	fliehen
	31. to lead	led	led	führen
	32. to leave	left	left	weggehen, verlassen
	33. to hold	held	held	halten
	34. to deal	dealt	dealt	handeln, sich befassen mit
	35. to mean	meant	meant	bedeuten
	36. to lean	leant	leant	(sich) lehnen
	37. to dream	dreamt	dreamt	träumen
	38. to read	read	read	lesen

GROUP 4 – LEARN (ALLE VERBEN DIESER GRUPPE GEHEN AUCH MIT -ED STATT MIT -T!)

*	39. to burn	burnt (burned)	burnt (burned)	(ver)brennen
	40. to learn	learnt (learned)	learnt (learned)	lernen
	41. to smell	smelt (smelled)	smelt (smelled)	riechen
	42. to spell	spelt (spelled)	spelt (spelled)	buchstabieren
	43. to spoil	spoilt (spoiled)	spoilt (spoiled)	verderben
	44. to spill	spilt (spilled)	spilt (spilled)	verschütten

GROUP 5 – SEND

	45. to bend	bent	bent	biegen, beugen
	46. to lend	lent	lent	(ver)leihen
	47. to send	sent	sent	schicken, senden
	48. to spend	spent	spent	*(Geld)* ausgeben; *(Zeit)* verbringen
*	49. to build	built	built	bauen

GROUP 6 – FIND

*	50. to find	found	found	finden
*	51. to bind	bound	bound	binden
	52. to grind	ground	ground	mahlen; schleifen
*	53. to wind	wound	wound	winden

GROUP 7 – THINK

*	54. to buy	bought	bought	kaufen
	55. to bring	brought	brought	bringen
*	56. to think	thought	thought	denken
	57. to fight	fought	fought	kämpfen
*	58. to catch	c*au*ght	c*au*ght	fangen
	59. to teach	t*au*ght	t*au*ght	lehren, unterrichten

GROUP 8 – WRITE

*	60. to drive	drove	driven	fahren
	61. to rise	rose	risen	aufgehen *(Sonne);* sich erheben
	62. to write	wrote	written	schreiben
	63. to ride	rode	ridden	reiten

GROUP 9 – SHOOT

*	64. to get	got	got	bekommen, werden
	65. to forget	forgot	forgotten	vergessen
	66. to shoot	shot	shot	schießen
	67. to shine	shone	shone	scheinen, glänzen
	68. to lose	lost	lost	verlieren

GROUP 10 – SPEAK

	69. to speak	spoke	spoken	sprechen
	70. to steal	stole	stolen	stehlen
	71. to break	broke	broken	(zer)brechen
	72. to freeze	froze	frozen	frieren, gefrieren
*	73. to wake up	woke up	woken up	aufwachen, -wecken
*	74. to tell	told	told	erzählen, sagen
	75. to sell	sold	sold	verkaufen
	76. to choose	chose	chosen	(aus)wählen

GROUP 11 – WEAR

	77. to wear	wore	worn	*(Kleider)* tragen
	78. to tear	tore	torn	zerreißen
	79. to swear	swore	sworn	schwören, fluchen
	80. to bear	bore	borne (born = geboren!)	ertragen

GROUP 12 – HIDE

	81. to hide	hid	hidden	(sich) verstecken
*	82. to bite	bit	bitten	beißen
	83. to light	lit (lighted)	lit (lighted)	anzünden
	84. to slide	slid	slid	gleiten, rutschen

GROUP 13 – 'W' VERBS

	85. to know	knew	known	kennen, wissen
*	86. to blow	blew	blown	wehen, blasen
*	87. to grow	grew	grown	wachsen, werden
	88. to throw	threw	thrown	werfen
*	89. to fly	flew	flown	fliegen
	90. to draw	drew	drawn	zeichnen; ziehen
*	91. to show	showed	shown	zeigen
*	92. to sow	sowed	sown	säen
	93. to sew	sewed	sewn	nähen
	94. to saw	sawed	sawn	sägen

GROUP 14 – CUT

95.	to bet	bet	bet	wetten
96.	to broadcast	broadcast	broadcast	senden, ausstrahlen *(Radio/TV)*
97.	to burst	burst	burst	bersten, platzen
98.	to cost	cost	cost	kosten
* 99.	to cut	cut	cut	schneiden
100.	to hit	hit	hit	treffen, schlagen
101.	to hurt	hurt	hurt	weh tun; verletzen
*102.	to let	let	let	(zu)lassen
*103.	to put	put	put	stellen, setzen, legen
104.	to set	set	set	setzen; untergehen *(Sonne)*
105.	to shut	shut	shut	schließen
106.	to spread	spread	spread	ausbreiten, ausdehnen; *(aufs Brot)* streichen
107.	to thrust	thrust	thrust	stoßen

GROUP 15 – AUXILIARY VERBS

*108.	to be	was / were	been	sein
*109.	to have	had	had	haben
*110.	to do	did	done	tun

GROUP 16 – REMAINING VERBS

* 111.	to make	made	made	machen
* 112.	to go	went	gone	gehen, fahren
* 113.	to come	came	come	kommen
114.	to become	became	become	werden
* 115.	to run	ran	run	laufen, rennen
* 116.	to see	saw	seen	sehen
* 117.	to hear	heard	heard	hören
* 118.	to give	gave	given	geben
119.	to forgive	forgave	forgiven	vergeben
120.	to forbid	forbade	forbidden	verbieten
* 121.	to say	said	said	sagen
122.	to pay	paid	paid	bezahlen
123.	to lay	laid	laid	legen
*124.	to lie	lay	lain	liegen
*125.	to sit	sat	sat	sitzen
126.	to stand	stood	stood	stehen
127.	to understand	understood	understood	verstehen
*128.	to beat	beat	beaten	schlagen
*129.	to take	took	taken	nehmen
*130.	to shake	shook	shaken	schütteln
* 131.	to eat	ate	eaten	essen
*132.	to fall	fell	fallen	fallen